peta

window

left

open

Books by Jennifer Grotz

Cusp
The Needle
Window Left Open

window
left
open

poems

Jennifer Grotz

Graywolf Press

This publication is made possible, in part, by the voters of Minnesota through a Minnesota State Arts Board Operating Support grant, thanks to a legislative appropriation from the arts and cultural heritage fund, and through a grant from the Wells Fargo Foundation Minnesota. Significant support has also been provided by Target, the McKnight Foundation, the Amazon Literary Partnership, and other generous contributions from foundations, corporations, and individuals. To these organizations and individuals we offer our heartfelt thanks.

Published by Graywolf Press
250 Third Avenue North, Suite 600
Minneapolis, Minnesota 55401

www.graywolfpress.org

Published in the United States of America

ISBN 978-1-55597-730-6

2 4 6 8 9 7 5 3 1
First Graywolf Printing, 2016

Library of Congress Control Number: 2015953590

Cover design: Jeenee Lee Design

Cover art: Dorota Mytych, *Everyday Insects*

for Ellen Bryant Voigt

Contents

window

left

open

one

The Forest

During the day I have watched them stand around and chew the yellow grass,
the longsuffering cows. Sometimes steam comes from their nostrils.
I have also visited them at night, seen an entire herd standing
in the rain, as unreacting as the trees behind them
when the jitter of flashlight warned of my approach.

Those were the cows in the field by the forest, and those
were the days when going outside felt like going inside.
There was the sound of a woodpecker pecking, and that was a kind of
knocking. And the sound of the pine trees creaking, and that was
a kind of door. And so you could enter the forest,
and although each moment you trespassed further
became more tense, it only lasted until you could no longer see the road.

Then you would be inside, on a kind of unending
staircase of roots worn silver like the soldered iron
that holds stained glass together. From a distance, it would be
mountains, but up close, under the arrows, spears, and ropes of trees,
it was a forest floor, palatial leaf-meal mosaics on the ground.
There was a little carpet of stream so clogged with leaves

it had stopped being a stream. And such a surfeit of silence,
it had become a kind of sound
to which, for a while, you could pay attention. Though
it's inaccurate, I want to say it was like staring at a light.
All you could do was sense it; then you had to recover,
by which I mean to wait for everything to grow dim again.
Then the mind was the only flashlight,
a little bobbing beam that would illuminate
randomly and too little.

Locked

And yes it is necessary to admit
walking in the forest
the heart is a lock

it has inviolable chambers
like the woods fallen trees

that block
access to the river
snowdrops surprising its edges
moss crystalline with frost

What I thought I wanted what I have tried to be
was the slender instrument that opened

a key   presence moving deeper into the forest
that releases the birds from the trees
and sends them   ascends them
to sky   by definition
open

but now there is nothing left to be solved like a riddle

this time the lock must be broken
what's left has to be seized

because God only loves the strong thief
I mean the man who breaks his heart for God

The Snow Apples

All fall their dropping was so insistent and
simultaneous on different branches it made
a syncopation. Now the end of February
and the snow apples that still hang
on otherwise bare branches,
why won't they let go?

               There's a stinging
sensation of cold on the skin, a singling
realization, a stuttering that outs itself, has it out
with itself *oh Lord I'll make a broken music or I'll die* . . .

Dulled, shrunken, nicked by wind-flung branches,
squirrel-pawed and beak-pierced, infested
macabre baubles hanging they are, it is—

a hard knot
deep in the core, something winter
winnows me down to. An uneasy seizing
that relaxes in the presence of sky.

The ones that fell have piled beneath the earth's pelt of snow—
the flesh inside them once white and wet as snow—
inedible and sad as the stones
on the lakeshore, pink or gray sandstone,
granite, rusted iron, eroded talc-smooth and uniform regardless—

Something gulped, indigestible—
something sad as the stones.

Snow

Rising as much as falling more mesmerizing than fire
when it lands it seems like dying because
when it's falling it's still alive

settling democratically on stone shoulders
underarms of branches but it sinks into absorbent moss
itself a kind of snow a saturated carpet so green

the eyes feast on it green
illuminating its own intricacy
miniature blades fronds needles bushy clumps

I don't understand growing up in the desert
how we ever kept time the wind let nothing accrue only the sun
gave us a psychedelic dust-infused nightly blaze

I never saw moss rarely saw rust jewel-colored cousins
moss grew on trees and there were no trees but rust
I looked for on metal that was everywhere gleaming

you could drive by whole fleets of cars and planes
parked in the desert to protect them from
the rust I longed to see the orange and purple

nowhere near all the oval windows with
no face waving good-bye the title of every day
of my childhood wandering would be

Landscape with No Human Figure in It since I myself was
the hungry lens but I don't mean to say still life
nature morte as the French call it there was life

～

in its tiny throes smaller even than mine lizards fire ants
snakes and groundhogs that lived underground
but I never saw snow didn't see rust only saw green imitations

of moss hot-glue-gunned on mother's cuckoo clock
or fuzzy-textured spray paint on a figurine but now
I know how moss floats treacherously

like a toupee covering a scalp of thick
mud my boots set into a slow motion of choppy waves
it's snowing hard now covering the moss

covering the mud there's a frenzied and
wavering synchronicity of flakes darting like fish
but snow differs it gets to swim in the sky

～

before it settles on surfaces and
I am lucky to have a desk by a window in winter
where falling snow entertains the mind the mind entering

the depths the layers the flakes I see in the distance a uniform haze
making the bare branches of trees more gray than brown
in the middle ground a zone of falling impossible

to absorb like a crowd interrupted
by zigzagging showoffs renegade flakes that zoom
surprisingly diagonally in front the true protagonists

of snow all three of these layered one in front of the other
like screens in a play a play about slowing time down to
something palpable or a song about what time does to man

less ominous later in the afternoon sun
when a dripping icicle keeps time like a metronome it's only
meaningless only harmless when nothing sticks to the ground

Snowflakes

Yesterday they were denticulate as dandelion greens, they
locked together in spokes and fell so weightlessly

I thought of best friends holding hands.
And then of mating hawks that soar into the air to link their claws

and somersault down, separating just before they touch the ground.
Sometimes the snowflakes glitter, it's more like tinkling

than snow, it never strikes, and I want to be struck, that is
I want to know what to do. I begin enthusiastically,

I go in a hurry, I fall pell-mell down a hill, like a ball of yarn's
unraveling trajectory—down and away but also surprising ricochets

that only after seem foretold. Yesterday I took a walk because
I wanted to be struck, and what happened was

an accident: a downy clump floated precisely in my eye.
The lashes clutched it close, melting it against the eye's hot surface.

And like the woman talking to herself in an empty church
eventually realizes she is praying, I walked home with eyes that melted snow.

On the Library Steps

The way the lips siphoned a stream into my lungs
and the body ever-so-subtly convulsed
in what was never actually pleasure but involuntary relief,
a shudder as poison moved steadily into the bloodstream,
so strong that the body mindlessly did it again, or the mind
bodilessly willed it again, then again, until the actual sensation
of smoking couldn't really be felt, and gray-brown clouds
filled the winter rooms, soaked into our coats and dresses.

That is what I remember this morning when I see
the leftover tobacco crumbles students stomped out
on the library steps, the abbreviated butts
excreting urine-colored stains into the snow,
the paper linings of filters all unglued,
pale and wet like raw calamari, and I suppose
there is a Buddhist click of recognition:

what I had desired had turned undesirable, yes,
and this ugly mess did not represent my sadness,
it only illustrated how catatonic it had become,
the mind numbly staring at it, and the convex globs
of spit nearby, not the sky, not the snow, gone
the reflex of shirking back. *Don't do it, just write it down,*
is what I had decided, but that just kept it lyric,
how I didn't want to live.
                              No attempt
in the poem for transcendence.
Just to lock up something wild.

Because a poem could still be good for
suffering. Choosing precisely how to.

The Whole World Is Gone

Driving alone at night, the world's pitch, black velvet
stapled occasionally by red taillights
on the opposite highway but otherwise mild
panic when the eyes' habitual check
produces nothing at all in the rearview mirror,
a black blank, now nothing exists
but the dotted white lines of the road,
and the car scissors the blackness open
like the mind's path through confusion,
but still no clarity, no arrival, only Pennsylvania darkness,
rocks, cliffs, vistas by day that thicken to black. It's
sensual, though, too, and interestingly mental. What
I do alone, loving him in my mind. Trying not to
let imagination win over reality. Hurtling through the night,
a passion so spent becomes a fact one observes. Not tempered,
just momentarily out of view by the body that perceives it.
So that if it desires, the mind can practice a prayer,
the one whose words begin: Deprive me.

Denial

Like a giant illuminated book, but with gold dust
hovering just above the pages, the glass cases house
butterfly wings, furred mummies of butterfly bodies,
butterfly antennae, and also moths,
humbler ones that look like they'd been found
in a junior high school, covered in dust
from the janitor's broom and smudges from
the math teacher's uncooperative piece of chalk.

In a room full of dead things, why can't I love what's alive?
I reach the glass case I'd had my back to and see
a still life of branches, but that's because
they'd spaced themselves exactly to appear as leaves,
and when one leaf starts to crawl atop another, I check
the sign: giant hissing cockroaches. I try

simply to watch them. But when an antenna begins
to flicker deliberately in surveillance, my body
shudders in a way it knows how to do
without me. Not a separation of mind and body, quite,
but neither a cooperation. There

my attention stalls until there's
a conversion into truth:
just as there are menial sins, and cardinal,
so there are the little and numerous and big and obvious
truths I deny. Let me start with the cockroaches.

Flat-backed, carapaced, geniusly engineered, how
quickly they skitter out of sight. Then wait
the way a mouse might, or a fox at the forest edge,
knowing most of the time we aren't paying attention at all.

Tears finally, in the parking lot,
head resting against the steering wheel
after my whole body fought for an hour against
the simple act of looking.
When will I get stronger? Is this how?

Listening

Water turns everything into a jewel
then puts a metal taste in the mouth
slowly replaced by dust. Which is why
standing in the rainy street
you feel much richer than you are. Or,
aware that everything will dry, much poorer.

You feel that way anyway in New York, and a little lost,
but let's be honest, that's what you want, to hide,
and like an owl, you've retreated not to high branches
but an anonymous sky-rise. And like the others who didn't flee,

you're up late waiting for the hurricane.
It's that usual hiss of nothing, of stillness, it's
the sound listening makes, and it slowly generates
the awareness of wind lashing outside, something like a fistfight
between rain and leaf, rain winning, leaves, twigs, whole branches
chipped away and blown down the street.

Seen from the seventh floor, looking down,
full shiny garbage bags piled symmetrically
become a cluster of grapes, trembling, until one gets plucked
by the wind. How straight the buildings stand, and how
elastic the trees, how mesmerizing to watch
how completely they will yield.

And the city streets are oddly empty
except for the monotonous bounce of a jogger
making his visual tick-tock toward the park,
or the dog-walker's vector from here to there
frustrated by his little lingering inspector.

When the raindrops start wholeheartedly,
stately at first as punctuation, how relieving it is,
now that you are listening this closely, now
that you can hear the rain-words
unraveling an epic discourse that seems
even as it calls you back to the window
to insist you will be exhausted if not asleep by the end.

Hangover in Paris

Sunlight hurts. My hair hurts.
My skin crawls as I come to realize where I am,

what I'm hearing. The *Salon de Tatouage*
next door, on Rue de la Roquette.
I'm awake enough to realize it, not enough to enjoy

how that sound (a bug zapper? a muffled drill?)
filters and grows metaphorical

while an artist and his client smoking in the courtyard
energetically debate
what the client will get inked into his arm.

I'm getting moody about permanence, not about
the weird abundance of the temporary, little mushrooms

that come up out of nowhere and disappear in a powdery puff
when stepped on accidentally. I think of *Nausea,*
when Sartre's character grows so disgusted

he writes in his journal: "Did nothing. Existed."
How maybe the former deprivation generates the latter.

How *in terms of the mythic, the historical,*
and of course the aesthetic, the two men have decided
on a spider. That ominously silent, eavesdropping creature.

Watchmaker

Something in the rented apartment
isn't working, the dying battery of an alarm
I can't locate, no fire, just a piercing shrill
every five minutes, time is not working and so,

sleepless, I'm existing in five-minute increments.
It is interesting, it is trying, I am trying
not to notice, or rather, to pay attention as I once did
entering the tiny watchmaker's shop in Krakow,

where every surface and wall was covered with
something ticking. I could feel my blood pressure rise
as I watched the watchmaker's calm, the precision
with his tweezers, the keen gaze through his monocle.

In Krakow, if a cat came up to me
I would speak to it in French sometimes by accident.
The beep is a reset button, it makes
my thinking start over, start on something new.

Why is it hard to remember to speak to animals
in their country's language? Once in France,
I spoke to an impudent peacock in English, not
because I forgot but to cut through any pretense.

No one ever speaks about how one's intimacy
grows confused in different languages, even
one's self, mildly at first, just briefly untethered,
you split yourself into two languages,

like the moment in a relationship
when you start to keep a secret.

Self-Portrait on the Street of an Unnamed Foreign City

The lettering on the shop window in which
you catch a glimpse of yourself is in Polish.

Behind you a man quickly walks by, nearly shouting
into his cell phone. Then a woman

at a dreamier pace, carrying a just-bought bouquet
upside down. All on a street where pickpockets abound

along with the ubiquitous smell of something baking.
It is delicious to be anonymous on a foreign city street.

Who knew this could be a life, having languages
instead of relationships, struggling even then,

finding out what it means to be a woman
by watching the faces of men passing by.

I went to distant cities, it almost didn't matter
which, so primed was I to be reverent.

All of them have the beautiful bridge
crossing a gray, nearsighted river,

one that massages the eyes, focuses
the swooping birds that skim the water's surface.

The usual things I didn't pine for earlier
because I didn't know I wouldn't have them.

I spent so much time alone, when I actually turned lonely
it was vertigo.

Myself estranged is how I understood the world.
My ignorance had saved me, my vices fueled me,

and then I turned forty. I who love to look and look
couldn't see what others did.

Now I think about currencies, linguistic equivalents, how lopsided they are,
while my reflection blurs in the shop windows.

Wanting to be as far away as possible exactly as much as still with you.
Shamelessly entering a Starbucks (free wifi) to write this.

Edinburgh Meditation

The painting is by Greuze, it's titled *A Boy with a Lesson-Book,*
but at first glance it's a girl, strawberry blond
with a lock of bangs pulled and knotted away from the pale brow.
And the pair of small perfect hands folded carefully
over the tiny lesson-book inadvertently causes tears
because they're painted so exactly the viewer recognizes them—
her little brother's, now grown and now
long passed away, like the boy in the painting—they belong to
the short-lived, ungendered beauty of a child being solemn.

The lesson-book's lettering, too, is painted with such precision
she's certain she could read it if only she could climb
atop some furniture and crook her head like a bird's—or
if she could just will herself to be the boy—both implausible
but in the quiet room of the museum on a winter morning,
only barely so in this thick dream of staring, the painting's
so convincing, that she could almost, in fact she lingers
a long time in that *almost,* but then she senses on her back
the eyes of the museum guard in his tartan pants,
and she's not one to make a scene.

Later, walking the moors, the boy's face will come back to her,
she will think of him while following footpaths
through the fields, rolling hills, woods, along the River Esk,
under stone bridges, alongside horses, and it will seem like
she is walking in a painting, tiny villages perched
in the distance, remote castles visible through late winter's
bare branches. How she loves the moors, they go on forever,
they go farther than her legs can walk, her mind can think,
they outlast her will, they outlast the daylight hours. Each time
she starts earlier, heads farther,

but the paths never end, she turns back when
the sun gets low and makes the hay seem to blaze,
burnishes the trees. Her steps, thousands
of them, start to feel like thinking's accrual
into knowledge, her eyes startled, hungrily observing details,
then recognition, then familiarity from repeated walks,
almost an ownership, because by now she's memorized the moors.

That's what the boy is doing in the painting,
the look in his eyes is one of trying to remember
something from the lesson-book his little hands
are covering. Verb conjugations, maybe, or vocabulary.
It looks like sadness, but it's simpler,
it's being lost, it's the boy running through the field
of his own mind. The longer she looks, the more somber
his eyes seem, and the flush in his left cheek is
not from winter's chill after walking the moors,
but emotion, and she begins to imagine him elsewhere,
about to descend a staircase, and solemnly,
absurdly announcing out loud but to no one,
"I regret the stairs."

She's picturing him at home, where a polite visitor asks
if he likes his new baby sister, and he shakes his head no
and exclaims, "All she does is cry!"
                                        When she looks at the painting,
it helps her remember what it was like to clasp her little brother's hands,
walk home with him from school. His fingernails always had
a little rind of dirt underneath, and so did their baby cousin's
on the Oklahoma reservation, and why
does she suddenly remember that, how the mother
gently trimmed the baby's nails with her teeth.

The woods are such a riot of branches, and the leaves
that fell in autumn are still on the ground, blanched
by decomposition's lace-making, and horseshoes emboss
the muddy parts of the path. Etiolated grasses,
spray of ferns, and in the wet shadowy spots, moss
flourishes so that green is practically a form of light,
and if she stays late on the path, she also sees
the sky's more sublime version of a screen-saver blue.

The silence of such places is so complete it sinks
into one's mind in waves, drenching it
with some life-giving essence, Edwin Muir once wrote, not
the mere absence of sound. In that silence
the moor is a living thing
spreading its fleece of purple and brown and green
to the sun. That's when she feels like she's
walking inside a painting, when it's either a secret
her every step helps discover or else a practice
of memory, she can't even tell. All she knows is that
she loves the boy's trance of concentration,
that momentary withdrawal where he listens
to an inner whisper, where his eyes perform that gesture
impossible to describe but recognized by a viewer
of being open but not seeing, emptying themselves
so as to hear.
                    Her neck begins to ache
because she's got it tilted, like Leonardo's Madonna in the next room,
she's been standing there gazing dreamily, so still, that
she has a quick sensation of *being* the painting, and the boy
being the world, the frame being the window through which

he could study her, also, if only he would finish his memorization,
if only he would raise his head up and look out:

                                                     wouldn't he see

she wants something she has no language for.
She doesn't want the language, she wants the something.

The Broom

Just jet lag, but these sleepless hours turn it
existential, that is, sad. Out of synch with time:
that's a man-made loneliness. It feels like
waiting to be let back in, but it's waiting for
something in me to change and until then,
it's lying upside down in the bed and hot, using
the blanket as a pillow, the pillow as a blanket.

Flutter of curtain in the blue light, the dry
sound of brushing from below, it's a broom on the sidewalk,
meticulously brushing clean my mind,
sloughing off everything that still clings.

I should be happy. On this fourth floor,
probably seventy-five feet in the air, I'm
at the altitude of the birds in the Pisgah Forest,
the ones that show how stirring it is
to live in the middle of the world, where there are
whole realms too high for humans, for animals,
too low for the tops of ambitious trees, just branches
to navigate through
                    exactly unlike an arrow,
trying never to reach a mark, just to fly gracefully above
the understory of rhododendron, the crinkled faces of the ferns,

the lake blurred, an oil painting stroked into relief
by insects, wind skimming the surface.

two

The Mountain

No matter how long I looked, I couldn't see it all,
much less understand it. Yes, I believed
the mountain could be understood,
that it was at least my task to try. It was a wall,

it was almost a painting, two-dimensional
from my window which served as picture frame.
I wasn't standing on the mountain, I was facing it.
From a window in a monastery on another mountain.

If I stood at the window and looked up,
which one cannot do in a painting, I saw
the mountain's top, the cloud-combed sky.
But this told me very little.

What my mind never tired of asking was the question
of how one could stand, where it was level enough to.
The trees seemed to cling, to grow sideways out of it,
from my distance, which only seemed very close

because there was nothing but air between us
and an unviewable valley below.
They looked undifferentiated, verdant as moss.
It was essentially a formal problem. How to look at

something too big for the frame. How the frame
made the concrete into something so abstract,
I had to will to see it for what it was.
I didn't love the mountain, but

I became very quiet when I was next to it.
I watched it turn from green to purple when
night's silks slinked up against it. I looked and looked. And still—
just to try to tell you what the sun did to it. And the clouds.

Scorpion

When it's warm, you'll see one every day,
Isabelle warns newcomers to the monastery. And so
I check my shoes, the bed, the pillow

until I find one. And the first scorpion was innocuous—
already dead, curled in the shower drain like a tuft of pubic hair.
The second, a closer call, balanced on the upturned
base of an espresso cup just washed.

Then a false alarm when an earwig crawled
from the center of a rose. There are roses
everywhere this time of year, it is natural
for the village women to collect downy piles into bowls,
then to press the petals like fingerprints into framed screens of fat.

So that when the roses are all gone, there will still be
the smell of rose petals, there will be the utterly pure because
thoroughly disembodied essence of rose,

persisting in the form of oil
which you may transfer to your own body,
rub and spread into thinner layers until the skin
absorbs the oil but leaves the short-lived essence of rose.

Now I've gone all day without one
and am afraid not for having found a scorpion
but from its very absence. All of the scorpions
purified into essence of scorpion, not a perfume
but a fear.

What amount of fear is the right amount of fear?
I want to find the correct proportion but
my only measure is analogy, to ponder
how this is like that. Sometimes I can see
there is no answer because
I am not asking the question right but
God, I am doing the best I know how.

Dragonfly and Wasp

I killed the wispy-winged things swarming
all over my pillow. But I let you be, dragonfly, you're
just neurotic, cautiously installed by the bedside lamp.
I admire your gauzy black-rimmed wings,
expressive antennae and tiny attentive eyes.
But with the lights off, you hurl yourself
about the room as if to crunch into a ball so
you can throw yourself away.

Involuntary as the twitch my lover makes
in sleep, releasing all the day's unused adrenalin.
Still it upsets me to hear you. I wish my fear was
as bumbling and unstinging as yours.

Something falls and falls inside me,
a glass jar breaks and spills.
And my fear is a depressed mother
still in her nightgown who doesn't
look down to see what crashed.
My fear: it won't even answer the phone.
"My" because I own it, the way one possesses a ghost.
Or a mother. And because it was never not there.
Last night I knew it was true, honest, and
the worst feeling imaginable.

Today it doesn't seem false, my despair, only premature.
The sun bakes the monastery stones
and loves the garden, loves the sunflowers ten feet tall,
invites the wasps back out. Slicing the air,
they come in one after another through the window,

then exit again, except for the one that lingers,
stirring something ominous into the afternoon.
Entering the wardrobe, not coming out.

They Come the Way Flowers Do

                              —late spring, on schedule,
and when they do for fifteen days
the mountains are littered with a beauty
humans hardly deserve, littered I say
because they perch right on the ground,
on the mountain face, and there is one so beautiful
I hope never to learn its name because
it appears as an unnamable marvel,
intricately tattooed upon a gray-blue wing,
the exact color of the slate rock that camouflages it.
But when it spreads its wings its back reveals
ecstatic blue, and when a dozen that waited like pebbles
for your approach alight, it is the opposite of snowfall,
butterflies hardly conjures how the world is snowing sky.

The Fog

Outside a gorgeous morning fog I stare at while
inside coffee spreads its alerting warmth and my mind
starts to soar, that sensation I have loved ever since, as a child,
I learned to read without moving my lips. Just in my mind!
How startling it was, like a radio or a river only I could hear.

Now it's how I can talk directly to you: oh fog, how I used to
watch you roll in on those spring mornings in Cassis, how
you could make the entire mountain outside my window disappear
and the whole world so visibly into a chamber of
such beautiful doubt that it would appall

when something so substantial as a bird would swoop out
and land on the terrace. Clarity, I suppose,
only comes when you leave but I love what soft featureless
comfort you are. And when you speak back, like the steam
I have watched in moments of perfectly useless concentration

emerge from the electric kettle on its way to climax,
a swirling atomic dust, particles
wobbling up out of the spout and then a thickening,
grainy as ash, and the force increasing and rising
high like the flame from an untrimmed wick and then

the curling plumes of voluptuous tresses of steam, thirty
seconds of such sensual escape!—
                                        A domestic iteration of what Jupiter said
to Io, I think, in the Correggio where he comes to her as a cloud and
the soles of her feet glow rosy as skin flushed after a hot bath.

I think I could stand a long time and watch the fog calling its visual whisper,
while I eat an orange, its rind suede-soft under my fingernails,
the smell it fills the room with the opposite of fog.

Just come closer, approach an eros you cannot enter,
try to find where I begin in the faint outlines of trees that from
where you stand now look like a smudge, look like something
once there but now erased, that is to say, look like the past.

Apricots

I judged them very carefully, as though
I'd been given the charge to determine
which are good or bad, and they were all good,
even the slightly overripe ones with bruises
had a bitter ferment that only brightened
the scent. And the too-young ones, firm
and slightly sour, not yet softened by the sun.
And the ripe ones, that felt like biting into
my own flesh, slightly carnivorous.

They had been elegant in the tree, tiny coquettes
blushing more and more until I picked them,
then they were minimalist and matte-colored
in wooden bowls, so barely furred one couldn't help
but clothe them, enclose them with your hand,
caress each one thoroughly before taking a bite,
exploring the handsome freckles left
from some minor blight.

Now I stand under the tree and
pluck them one after the other.
Each one tastes different, like a mind having
erratic thoughts. Going into the trance
halfway between eating and thinking,
the thought of an apricot, the apricot of a thought,
whose goodness occurs over time, so that
some had been better earlier, others soon
would become correct, I mean ripe.

Sundials

They do not make a shape themselves, which is why
they look like marks left from something sliced,
but the sun doesn't slice, and that is what they measure,
these lines, on every wall of the courtyard so that the Franciscans

could know as precisely as possible the time to ring the bells.
Humans invented time, and this morning, watching
the sun's shadow slice across the walls, I think they did so
as a form of praise. Nature made the flowers

smell beautiful to attract the creatures that pollinate them.
Except for the dandelions, too many to count, left for the wind
to pollinate instead. What sparrows are to birds, little wisps, half-bald now
after the rain, past the days they lit entire fields a solar yellow.

Little lampposts of the field, little clocks. That's what happens
after staring at the sundials frescoed on the monastery walls.
Everything becomes one: the lizards in the morning heat flicker
like second hands all over the walls, little gray lightning bolts.

The roses measure the amount of time we can bear
their beauty, and the candelabra measures the length of dinner on the grass.
The trees are clocks for the wind, and the cherries are clocks for the birds,
and the pupils are clocks that measure one's affection

but can be read only by the other, the *affected*. Vaster: the mountains
measure the clouds and the dandelions in the field measure how far
the wind travels, how far it carries the seeds, while the spider
in the corner of my room is the second hand to stillness.

And the poem is a clock that measures the time and the time
it takes me to comprehend this, the time and the weather.

A Poem about a Peacock

I can't decide what the poem should be about: its cry, so
awful, like the hilarious encounter of two toddlers
with pants puffy over diapers
discovering they are conversant in squeal
if not words,
                while that plumage unfans
black pearls opalescing purple, green, blue in the sun,
spells out eyes—how literally they say *look at me*—

or whether I should contemplate here, joyously, gratefully
the fact that there are peacocks!

How did I forget?
                    And what to make of my conflicted delight
in that borderline-sublime when one is stalled
from judgment and simply pays bewildered attention.
This peacock is stranger than Mt. Rushmore.

I curl my fingers around the chicken-wire mesh
while he calms down again,
dragging behind his psychedelic ponytail of feathers.
So far from the grace of the blackbird or
the elegance of the eagle hovering beautifully in the sky,
the white flash of underside
like the metallic gleam of fish changing direction.

Which brings the question of how far
should the poem wander? Can I tell how this peacock
struts in his little yard, performing for the peahen
who runs away, but also how this domestic scene takes place
on the lush green steppe of a tiered garden of a sixteenth-century monastery

built right into the solid rock of the Alps?
                                    And should the poem
zoom out to history? For the peacock is only here
because castles and monasteries always had peacocks, just look at
the frescoes in the refectory.
                            Or does the poem zoom into the personal?
That, gentle reader, your lens for the poem walks back and forth,
from the peacock to the rose bushes, from the clothesline to the fishpond,
from the frescoes to the, let's be honest, always disappointing European plumbing.

What am I to make of him?
The whole rest of the world is still waiting to be encountered.
But wherever I go in this poem, there's a peacock.

Cherries

What might be universally beautiful is hard to imagine,
perhaps only the sunrise and sunset,
perhaps the moon. If on earth

it might be cherries,
loved by the fierce and tender, eaten
by birds and foxes, and what humans don't take
are claimed by little green worms.

It's the time of year everyone stops what they're doing to eat them.
Pits bundled in animal scat nestle between cobblestones.
For these few weeks they gleam in every tree
the whole world seems not only edible but delicious.

Is there a pleasure in the mind like this simple sugar,
cherry joy—the whole mouth involved in

plucking the fruit from the resistant stem,
tongue, teeth, and lips cooperating in slipping the sweet flesh
englobing the pit, wet, belly-beautiful

in the mouth able to
collect and hold two or three in one cheek before
spitting them out. Nothing is more true than the body
then, how it is made to consume pleasure, for pleasure
to pass right through. It's the mind that's

made to ponder it, to hold on. The mind of Japanese samurai
held the cherry as an emblem for the warrior, he who
breaks the skin and sheds the flesh and blood
to find the stone within.

I have watched the cherries turn from pale yellow to dark as olives,
I have picked them straight from the tree, red and obvious from afar
but up close hiding between lush leaves, little clumps of them,

I have used a ladder for what I could not reach
and for those even higher, I beat against the branches
until a cherry rain pelted down. I have picked up caved-in,
oozing rotten ones in search of the sturdy that have fallen.

And I have savored the brown rustle
that dissolves in the fingers reminding that each one was
a flower first, but that's all I want of

memory, I think, the distorting entrails of the mind.
Or so I resolve until I'm sated. Until I'm
staring into the night. Then I'm eager to pluck the stars.

The Piano on Top of the Alps

Not the one Mr. Cogito contemplates, but a real one,
and on its way back down now, the concert over,
musicians long gone and the crowd who came to hear,
even the firmament above the monastery
dissipated in sunlight's humid haze, stars in hiding.

Also the two men who accompany it, one young,
the other not, and the motorized conveyor
the piano, turned sideways, is strapped to,
a sort of mini-bulldozer meant to negotiate
the seventeen thousand cobble-bumps of terrain
they must descend. One man sweating on each end,
their palms slipping on the piano's impossible black sheen.
Strapped on top, in surrender, the piano bench legs point skyward.

And the unnatural tracks
this procession leaves behind
of fallen figs, crushed
leaves, perfectly flattened circles
of animal feces.

Not sounding a note, but here the piano is, still meaning something,
still, most of all, heavy and hot and requiring careful attention.

And once back down on the quotidian earth
maybe, like a foreign receipt unearthed in a pocket,
it will emit some molecule of exalted air.

Or some drop, the way Alpine snow eventually melts
and rolls down to the world in bottles of Evian.
And the world so thirsty after ecstasy.

Window Left Open

All you have to do is open the window
to let the night in: then moths
effervesce in a stream

toward the lamp, then the cool air
that blows between the blackbird and
the bat, air that blues the whole world

lets itself in, the whole world
stared at so intently even in the dark
by the baby marguerites growing

straight out of the rock walls,
white, pink, fuchsia, with yellow bristled centers.
What do daisies see with their feathery eye?

Not the night air though it blooms, too,
because it wants to be seen. It borrows the moths.
Half-asleep, but never asleep, I see

what they are: perched tightly together like carnations,
a fidgeting corsage of little engines. Or words
the lamp knows how to translate

from the teeming night. That's what I ask for next, God,
that's why I'll let myself sleep:
translate me.

Poppies

There is a sadness everywhere present
but impossible to point to, a sadness that hides in the world
and lingers. You look for it because it is everywhere.
When you give up, it haunts your dreams
with black pepper and blood and when you wake
you don't know where you are.

But then you see the poppies, a disheveled stand of them.
And the sun shining down like God, loving all of us equally,
mountain and valley, plant, animal, human, and therefore
shouldn't we love all things equally back?
And then you see the clouds.

The poppies are wild, they are only beautiful and tall
so long as you do not cut them,
they are like the feral cat who purrs and rubs against your leg
but will scratch you if you touch back.
Love is letting the world be half-tamed.
That's how the rain comes, softly and attentively, then

with unstoppable force. If you
stare upward as it falls, you will see
falling sparks that light nothing only because
the ground interrupts them. You can hear the way they'd burn,
the smoldering sound they make falling into the grass.

That is a sound for the sadness everywhere present.
The closest you have come to seeing it
is at night, with the window open and the lamp on,
when the moths perch on the white walls,
tiny as a fingernail to large as a Gerber daisy,
and take turns agitating around the light.

If you grasp one by the wing,
its pill-sized body will convulse
in your closed palm and you can feel the wing beats
like an eyelid's obsessive blinking open to see.
But now it is still light and the blackbirds are singing,
their voices the only scissors left in this world.

Notes

The last lines of "Locked" are improvised from "The Strong Thief" in Martin Buber's *Tales of the Hasidim*.

"The Snow Apples" quotes in italics from Theodore Roethke's poem, "In Evening Air."

"Listening" is for Lillie Robertson.

"The Piano on Top of the Alps" is a felicitous response to Zbigniew Herbert's poem "Mr. Cogito and the Imagination," which contains an imaginary piano on the top of the Alps as a figure for exalted poetry.

Acknowledgments

Many of the poems in this manuscript have appeared previously in journals, sometimes in slightly differing versions. I would like to thank the editors who selected these poems:

The Academy of American Poets *Poem-A-Day:* "The Whole World Is Gone" and "Self-Portrait on the Street of an Unnamed Foreign City"

The American Poetry Review: "Cherries" and "Locked"

Copper Nickel: "Hangover in Paris"

The Cortland Review: "Denial," "On the Library Steps," and "The Broom"

The Florida Review: "The Mountain"

New England Review: "Poppies," "Sundials," "A Poem about a Peacock," "The Forest," "The Fog," "Snowflakes," "Scorpion," "Dragonfly and Wasp," and "Listening"

The New Republic: "Window Left Open"

The New Yorker: "Apricots"

Poetry International: "Watchmaker"

"Poppies" also appeared in *The Best American Poetry 2011,* edited by Kevin Young, with series editor David Lehman, published by Scribner.

"Poppies" also appeared in the *Paris Review*'s "The Poem Stuck in My Head" feature, selected by Ta-Nehisi Coates.

"Poppies" also appeared in *The Rag-Picker's Guide to Poetry: Poems, Poets, Process*, edited by Eleanor Wilner and Maurice Manning, published by University of Michigan Press.

I am particularly grateful to the Monastère de Saorge, located in the French Alpes-Maritimes, which inspired much of this book and is where many of these poems were conceived. I would also like to thank Hawthornden Castle in Scotland and the Maison Dora Maar for their generosity of time and support that enabled the completion of this book.

Jennifer Grotz is the author of two previous poetry collections, *The Needle* and *Cusp*. She teaches at the University of Rochester and in the low-residency MFA program at Warren Wilson College, and she serves as the assistant director of the Bread Loaf Writers' Conference.

The text of *Window Left Open* is set in Adobe Caslon. Book design by Rachel Holscher. Composition by Bookmobile Design & Digital Publisher Services, Minneapolis, Minnesota. Manufactured by Thomson-Shore on acid-free, 30 percent postconsumer wastepaper.